P. 10

21st Century Skills Library

HEALTH AT RISK

SMOKING

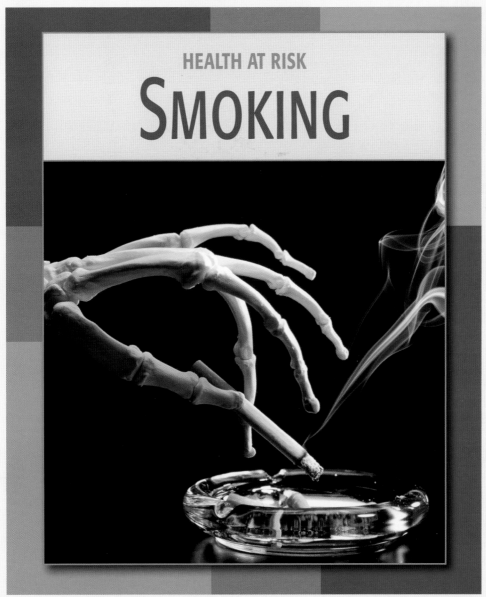

Heather Miller

Cherry Lake Publishing
Ann Arbor, Michigan

CHERRY LAKE
Publishing

Published in the United States of America by Cherry Lake Publishing
Ann Arbor, Michigan
www.cherrylakepublishing.com

Content Advisor: Carolyn Walker, RN, PhD, Professor, School of Nursing, San Diego
State University, San Diego, California

Photo Credits: Cover and page 1, © Oscar Burriel/Photo Researchers, Inc.; page 4,
© S. Terry/Photo Researchers, Inc.; page 7, © Phanie/Photo Researchers, Inc.; page 9,
© PSL Images/Alamy; page 10, Maury Aaseng; page 13, Dr. P. Marazzi/Photo
Researchers, Inc.; page 14, © Photofusion Library/Paul Baldesare/Alamy; page 17,
AP Images/Beth A. Keiser; page 19, © Sherrie Smith/Shutterstock; page 22, © LEDPIX/
Alamy; page 24, AP Images/Mickey Krakowski; page 26, AP Images/Matt York; page 28,
© Paul Reid/Shutterstock

Library of Congress Cataloging-in-Publication Data
Miller, Heather.
 Smoking / Heather Miller.
  p. cm.—(Health at risk)
Includes index.
ISBN-13: 978-1-60279-286-9
ISBN-10: 1-60279-286-0
1. Tobacco—Physiological effect—Juvenile literature. 2. Smoking—Juvenile literature.
3. Tobacco use—Juvenile literature. I. Title. II. Series.
RA1242.T6M55 2008
613.85—dc22   2008017501

Cherry Lake Publishing would like to acknowledge the work of
The Partnership for 21st Century Skills.
Please visit www.21stcenturyskills.org *for more information.*

TABLE OF CONTENTS

CHAPTER ONE

A Dangerous Habit

Studies have shown that the younger a person is when he or she starts smoking, the more it becomes a lifelong habit.

Sarah battled cancer as a baby. With treatment, she got better. But having cancer once didn't stop her from risking her health by smoking cigarettes. She knew smoking was harmful. Even so, while in high school in Stockton, California, Sarah smoked a pack a day. "When you're addicted to cigarettes, you can rationalize anything. Now I look back and think I must have been crazy," she says.

Smoking is a dangerous habit. Almost all people who use tobacco become addicted to **nicotine**. Nicotine is a poisonous chemical found in tobacco. When you inhale cigarette smoke, nicotine enters your lungs. There it's absorbed by the blood. And then it's carried through your body. Nicotine reaches your brain eight seconds after the first cigarette puff. It makes you feel good right away. You might feel like you have a lot of energy. Or you might feel calm. But the good feelings caused by smoking don't last. They soon fade and you long for another cigarette. The urge to smoke can be very strong. Soon it takes more and more nicotine to get a good feeling from smoking.

21st Century Content

Smoking is a big problem all over the world. About 15 billion cigarettes are sold worldwide each day. The number of smokers in the United States and Canada is falling. But smoking is on the rise in some other countries. In China, 54 percent of the male population smokes. In the Philippines, 50 percent of adult males smoke and so do an alarming 37 percent of young males. Use the Internet to find statistics about cigarette use in three different countries. Compare smoking rates from 10 years ago, 5 years ago, and today. Where are smoking rates rising or falling the fastest? How do the numbers for men compare with the numbers for women?

People who start smoking often keep smoking for many years. That's because nicotine is so addictive. The average smoker smokes between 5 and 15 cigarettes each day. That's almost 5,500 cigarettes each year!

More than 45 million adults smoke in the United States. That's 21 percent of the adult population. In Canada, the percentage is slightly lower. There, 15 percent of adults say they are regular smokers. Studies show that there are more male smokers than female smokers. But the difference is very slight.

The harms of smoking are well known. Yet every day young people try cigarettes for the first time. And many

Many smokers admit that it is a dangerous and dirty habit. But it is also a very difficult habit to break.

keep smoking. One 2007 survey found that 46 percent of U.S. teens have smoked cigarettes at least once by their senior year in high school. Twenty-two percent of 12th-graders and 14 percent of 10th-graders have smoked in the past 30 days. Even 22 percent of 8th-graders say they've tried cigarettes at least once. Seven percent say

they've tried cigarettes in the last 30 days. Teenage smoking is a problem in Canada too. One survey found that 15 percent of Canadian teens are regular smokers. Nine percent of those say they smoke every day.

Health officials worry about teenage smoking. Teens who smoke often become lifelong smokers. Lifelong smokers are more likely to develop serious health problems.

CHAPTER TWO

CHEMICAL STICKS

A cigarette labeled "poison" warns that it harms human health. Fifty of the more than 4,000 chemicals in cigarettes can cause cancer.

Nicotine is a strong poison found in cigarettes. But it is not the only poison you inhale when smoking. Over 4,000 chemicals can be detected in cigarettes or cigarette

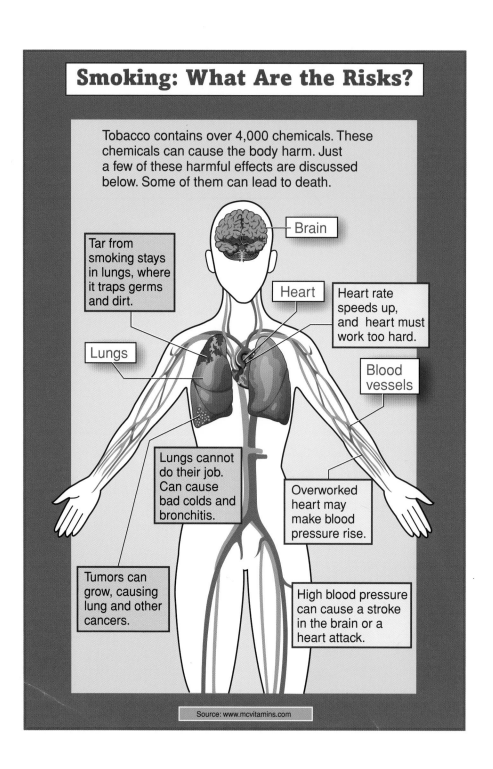

Smoking: What Are the Risks?

Tobacco contains over 4,000 chemicals. These chemicals can cause the body harm. Just a few of these harmful effects are discussed below. Some of them can lead to death.

Brain

Tar from smoking stays in lungs, where it traps germs and dirt.

Heart

Heart rate speeds up, and heart must work too hard.

Lungs

Blood vessels

Lungs cannot do their job. Can cause bad colds and bronchitis.

Overworked heart may make blood pressure rise.

Tumors can grow, causing lung and other cancers.

High blood pressure can cause a stroke in the brain or a heart attack.

Source: www.mcvitamins.com

smoke. Over 50 of these are known to cause cancer. One powerful poison found in cigarettes is arsenic. Arsenic has been known as a deadly poison for over 500 years. Another is sulfuric acid. It is known to harm the lungs if inhaled. Ammonia is another **toxic** chemical. It is added to cigarettes to boost nicotine's effect. Methoprene is also found in cigarettes. It is also used in products made for killing insects. The risks of smoking are great. But the strong urge to smoke makes smokers take in small doses of poison each day.

Smoking is bad for others as well as the smoker. A pregnant woman who smokes can harm her child. Studies show that babies born to women who smoke are more likely to have low birth weight. A baby with low birth weight is more likely to have serious health problems. These include cerebral palsy and mental retardation. Even normal-weight babies can be affected by smoking. Those whose mothers smoke have a 33 percent higher chance of dying shortly before or after birth than babies whose mothers don't smoke. Groups such as the March of Dimes work to improve babies' health. They teach women about the effects of smoking on their babies. They hope that women will decide not to smoke once they have this information. The group's yearly March for Babies raises money and awareness. Check to see how you can get involved with this or other programs in your area.

Putting poison in your body causes great harm. Over 400,000 people in the United States die each year from health problems related to smoking. Smoking is a factor in more deaths than AIDS, car accidents, drug overdoses, fires, suicides, and homicides combined. Cancer, stroke, emphysema, and heart disease are a few of the illnesses linked to smoking.

People with illnesses related to smoking suffer greatly. Emphysema is a lung disease. People who have this disease have trouble breathing. Even doing simple daily activities can be a struggle.

The California Department of Public Health tries to get people to stop smoking. In one TV ad, the department shows how smoking and lung disease are connected. In this ad, a young smoker who seems healthy speaks. He says, "I can't go more than a few hours

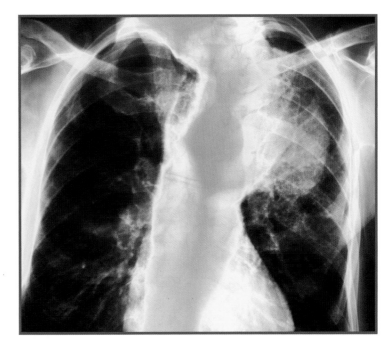

These lungs are from a 70-year-old woman. The yellow parts are cancerous. Symptoms of lung cancer include a cough due to chronic bronchitis, chest pain, and coughing up blood.

without a cigarette." He is answered by a dying patient. That patient whispers, "I can't go more than a few feet without an oxygen tank."

Experts say that smoking can shorten a person's life by about 10 years. The longer you smoke, the higher the risk that your life will be cut short.

CHAPTER THREE

WHY PEOPLE SMOKE

There are as many reasons that people give for having started smoking as there are smokers. Most agree, however, that they wish they had never started.

People start smoking for different reasons. Some people think smoking will give them energy. Others think smoking will reduce stress or help them lose weight. Many teenagers smoke because they think it will make them look older or cooler. Still others smoke simply because their friends smoke.

Cindy T. of Mountain View, Missouri, says her dad was a smoker. As a fifth-grader, she hid cigarettes in a school bathroom. Then she would smoke with her friends. Now an adult, she says, "I ended up spending approximately thirty thousand dollars on cigarettes before I could finally kick the habit."

Tobacco companies are also blamed for encouraging people to smoke. This has led to limits on ads for cigarettes. Canada has banned cigarette ads. The United States restricts ads but does not ban them. In the United States, cigarette ads are not allowed on TV or radio. They

are also banned from some magazines found in school libraries. But cigarette makers may run ads on billboards, in other magazines, and on vending machines.

Cigarette companies spend over $12 billion per year to promote their products. Tobacco companies know that most lifelong smokers start smoking as teens. So, they sponsor sporting events that young people enjoy. Or they create flashy ads that appeal to teens. Some sell cigarettes in flavors such as chocolate, lime, and toffee. Critics say that flavored cigarettes target teens. They say that cigarette makers use flavors and colorful packaging to make smoking seem

A cigarette ad promotes smoking as healthy and outdoorsy. Some experts believe that such ads entice people to try smoking.

harmless and fun. Cassandra Welch of the American Lung Association says, "Caribbean Chill? Mocha mint? These sound like ice creams to me, not something that kills you.

It's just a way to addict young people." Tobacco companies say that they are just trying to offer people who already smoke more choices.

There is no single reason why people start smoking. Tobacco companies may tempt more young people to smoke. Teenagers do indeed choose to smoke on their own. No matter why they start, the choice will cost them their health.

CHAPTER FOUR

TIME TO QUIT

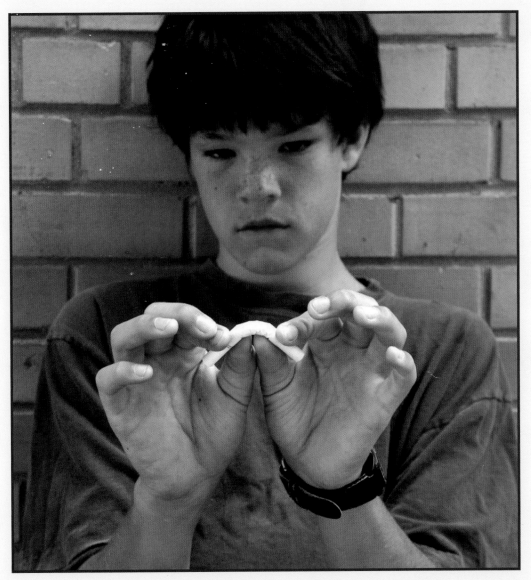

At least one teen decides against smoking his first cigarette. Many teens start smoking because a peer encourages them to try it.

Life & Career Skills

Nicotine is said to be as addictive as the illegal drug heroin. No wonder so many people struggle to kick the habit. Test your own willpower. Try to give up something you enjoy. How many days can you go without eating french fries, ice cream, or candy? The cravings you experience for these things may seem strong. But they are mild compared with a nicotine craving.

Once a person becomes addicted to smoking, it is very hard to stop. A smoker's brain and body get used to the nicotine. This means that a smoker must keep smoking just to feel normal. Without cigarettes, smokers quickly start to feel bad. Smokers crave nicotine. They may feel irritable or anxious. They may also feel depressed, restless, or hostile. They often crave food, overeat, and gain weight. Smokers know that one more cigarette will get rid of these bad feelings. And that makes it hard for them to stay away from nicotine.

When a smoker decides to quit, it's no easy task. Nicotine addiction is one of the hardest addictions to break. Many programs give smokers who are trying to quit tips to boost their willpower. The American Heart Association suggests that smokers track their progress. They can do this by writing down the time and place of every cigarette they smoke. The American Lung Association offers an online support program.

Some smokers need more help. Many do better if they stop smoking a little at a time. These smokers sometimes turn to products that give the body small amounts of nicotine. These products come in different forms. They include nasal sprays, patches that stick to the skin, chewing gums, and inhalers. Some smokers rely on these products to reduce the symptoms of sudden withdrawal. Allen Carr started smoking at 18. He smoked heavily for 33 years: "I smoked a hundred a day on a bad day, and never fewer than sixty." After some early failures, he finally quit smoking. He tried to help others to do the same until his

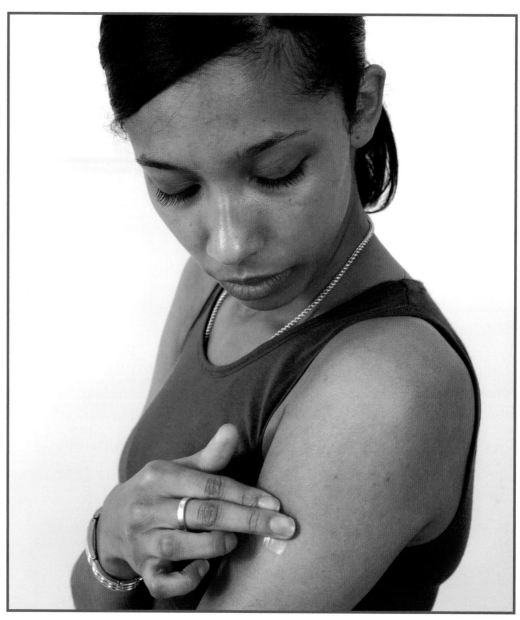

A woman applies a nicotine patch to keep herself from smoking. Many such non-smoking aids become a crutch, with people becoming as addicted to the aid as to smoking.

death from lung cancer in 2006. Carr wrote books about his experience. He also founded clinics to show smokers how to quit for good and to inspire nonsmokers not to start.

CHAPTER FIVE

CLEAN THE AIR

An anti-smoking ad by the American Lung Association uses the popular "Joe Camel" character to give the other side of smoking.

Many groups work to spread knowledge about the dangers of cigarettes. The prevention of teenage smoking is a high priority. The American Lung Association, for instance, sponsors the N-O-T (Not-On-Tobacco) program. This 10-session program tries to help teens who want to quit smoking. At each session, teen smokers learn new ways to deal with stress and peer pressure. The goal is for them to be able to set aside their cigarettes for good.

Some middle and high schools invite public speakers to talk to teens about smoking. Most public speakers have a personal or family connection to smoking. They tell dramatic stories of health problems and struggles. Patrick Reynolds often speaks to students. He is the grandson of R.J. Reynolds, founder of the giant R.J. Reynolds Tobacco Company. Reynolds's grandfather and oldest brother died from diseases linked to smoking. Now he travels the country to tell his family's story and to urge kids not to smoke.

The grandson of cigarette magnate R.J. Reynolds talks to students, urging them not to smoke.

Other antismoking speakers show students exactly what smoking does to people. At Roosevelt Elementary School in Mankato, Minnesota, a speaker showed students two real lungs. The first one belonged to a nonsmoker. It appeared pink and healthy. The second came from a smoker's body. It was black and misshapen from years of smoking damage. Students who saw the lungs were disgusted by the damaged tissue. At the end of his presentation, the speaker asked the students to sign a contract stating they would never smoke cigarettes.

Many other efforts are aimed at clearing the air of secondhand smoke. Thirty-five states have laws that limit

Ninety percent of long-term smokers begin using cigarettes before age 21. Many groups offer programs to help teens stay away from cigarettes. Does your school have a program to help prevent smoking? If so, find out what information is presented. If not, contact your local branch of the American Lung Association, the American Heart Association, or the American Red Cross. Find out if they can bring a program to your school.

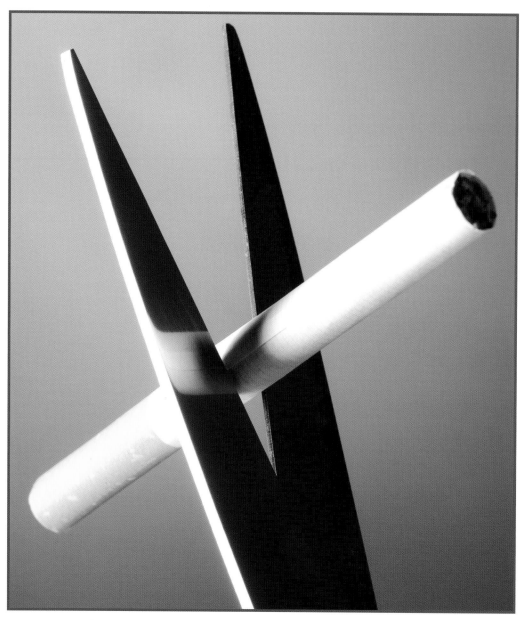

Eliminating cigarettes is the first step to quitting but avoiding them in the first place is the best way to avoid smoking's dangers.

smoking in workplaces and public spaces. These include restaurants, bars, and bowling alleys. And some major hotel chains now ban smoking too.

The best way to avoid the health risks of smoking is to stay away from cigarettes. Cigarettes are poisonous. One puff could lead to a lifetime of addiction and sickness.

21st Century Content

Some large cities have banned smoking in bars and restaurants. New York City is one of these. Minnesota approved a different type of ban. In 2007 it banned smoking on public transit and in private workplaces. Many people argue that antismoking laws violate personal freedom. Some argue that these laws are OK for government buildings. But they think that private businesses such as restaurants should be free to allow smoking if they want. Use the Internet to find arguments to support different views on this issue. With which view do you agree most? Why?

GLOSSARY

anxious (ANK shuss) uneasy or worried; fearful of what might happen

cerebral palsy (SER uh brawl PALL zee) a disorder caused by a brain injury resulting in poor muscle control. Premature and low-birth-weight babies have a higher risk of cerebral palsy.

emphysema (em fuh SEE muh) a lung disease in which air spaces in the lungs become damaged or scarred. With emphysema, breathing is difficult and the body does not get enough oxygen.

hostile (HOSS tl) unfriendly and aggressive

inhalers (in HAY lerz) devices that deliver medicine to the lungs as a fine spray that is breathed into the nose or mouth

nicotine (NIK uh teen) a poisonous substance found in tobacco; the main addictive ingredient in cigarettes

secondhand smoke (se KUND hand smoke) environmental tobacco smoke; a mix of smoke given off by the tips of burning cigarettes and smoke exhaled by nearby smokers

stroke (stroke) interruption of blood flow to the brain, causing damage to brain cells; possible results are permanent disability and death. Smoking increases the risk of stroke.

toxic (TOX ik) poisonous

For More Information

Books

Hudson, David L. *Smoking Bans*. New York: Chelsea House, 2004.

Hyde, Margaret O., and John F. Setaro. *Smoking 101: An Overview for Teens*. Minneapolis: Twenty-First Century, 2005.

Koss, Amy Goldman. *Smoke Screen*. Middleton, WI: American Girl, 2000.

Sanders, Bruce. *Let's Talk About Smoking*. Corona, CA: Stargazer, 2005.

Stewart, Gail B. *Smoking*. Detroit, MI: Kidhaven, 2002.

Web Sites

Tobacco Free Kids-Gallery of Cigarette Advertisements
www.tobaccofreekids.org/adgallery/index.php3?Country=1
This Web site offers hundreds of cigarette advertising examples from all over the world.

Mayo Clinic—10 Ways to Help Teens Stay Smoke-Free
www.mayoclinic.com/health/teen-smoking/HQ00139
This page lists ways to help keep kids and teens from taking even one puff of a cigarette.

Nemours Foundation, KidsHealth.com—Smoking
www.kidshealth.org/teen/drug_alcohol/tobacco/smoking.html
Read the many ways smoking can harm you and your health.

Quit Smoking Support—Teenagers Smoking Section
www.quitsmokingsupport.com/teens.htm
Visit this Web site to see photos of healthy and diseased human lungs.

INDEX

ABOUT THE AUTHOR

Heather Miller lives in northeast Indiana, where she works as both a writer and an art teacher. She enjoys writing nonfiction books as well as picture books. She loves to teach through her writing and strives to inspire her readers to investigate and learn about their world.